THE   BEATITUDES

B^{The}eatitudes
Pattern for Christian Living

Helen Cecilia Swift, SND deN

ALBA · HOUSE · NEW · YORK

SOCIETY OF ST. PAUL. 2187 VICTORY BLVD., STATEN ISLAND, NEW YORK 10314

Library of Congress Cataloging-in-Publication Data

Swift, Helen.
    The Beatitudes : pattern for Christian living / by Helen Cecilia
Swift.
        p.   cm.
  ISBN: 0-8189-0592-1
  1. Beatitudes — Devotional literature.   2. Christian life — Catholic
authors. I. Title.
BT382.S85   1990
241.5'3—dc20   90-41241
                                                  CIP

Designed, printed and bound in the United States of
America by the Fathers and Brothers of the
Society of St. Paul, 2187 Victory Boulevard,
Staten Island, New York 10314, as part of their
communications apostolate.

Printing Information:

Current Printing - first digit   2 3 4 5 6 7 8 9 10 11 12

Year of Current Printing - first year shown

1993   1994   1995   1996   1997

TABLE OF CONTENTS

INTRODUCTION

*I*n his Gospel, Matthew wrote that early in Jesus' public life, "When Jesus saw the crowds, he went up the mountain, and after he had sat down, his disciples came to him. He began to teach them" (Mt 5:1-2). His teaching that day is summarized in the eight statements we have come to call the "Beatitudes."

It is very easy for us today to disregard the Beatitudes as too idealistic for our *real* world. They *are* ideals that draw and challenge us to a full Christian life. Jesus was not stating a new moral code to replace the Ten Commandments, nor enunciating optional virtues from which we can pick and choose. Rather, Jesus was revealing a new way of life grounded in reliance on God and expressing the values of a true disciple.

Now, two thousand years later, the Beatitudes remain the inner attitudes modern disciples struggle to express in their lives. They can never be fully attained or they would not be ideals. Through striving for these ideals, individuals fulfill their human potential and help to spread the reign of God in the world.

Throughout the history of Christianity books, sermons, homilies, and meditations have attempted to interpret the Beatitudes and motivate Christians to live them. So why another book on the subject?

This book aims to show that the Beatitudes speak very forcibly to the problems of modern society. It is based on the conviction that the message of Jesus is meaningful for every time and place but needs to be constantly reinterpreted in the light of new understandings. For example, archaeological discoveries provide a deeper understanding of ancient languages, leading to new insights into Scripture. Also, advancement in the various branches of psychology contribute new knowledge of the inner dynamics of the human person. With new knowledge and deeper insights, each generation must ask itself, "What do the Beatitudes say to our generation about the Christian life?" In this way, the Beatitudes are new for each generation as people look for meaning and motivation in their lives.

However, the interpretation for today's world must begin by understanding the context in which Jesus presented the Beatitudes. In Matthew's Gospel, the first two verses of Chapter 5, which introduce the Beatitudes, are highly symbolic. It is clear that many more people were present than the twelve apostles. Jesus responded to the presence of the crowd that was following him by going up the mountain.

Among the Jews and other religious groups, there was a common understanding that a mountain was the dwelling place of the deity. They challenged one another — "*Our God* lives on the *highest* mountain" implying, "*Our God* is the greatest, most powerful, most majestic!" Therefore, going up the mountain, symbolized a desire to get closer to God. Jesus' action of climbing the mountain was an invitation to the people to move into a closer relationship with God.

When Jesus sat down the people knew immediately that he was going to teach them for rabbis always sat among their disciples. Men, women and children took their places at the feet of Jesus and waited eagerly to hear his words.

There are two words in the Beatitudes that often give people problems: "blessed" and "kingdom." In the Hebrew, the word "blessed" is an exclamation, "O Blessed!" So Jesus was not pronouncing blessings on his disciples but exclaiming how blessed they were. They were blessed because they wanted to follow him, and were therefore part of the Kingdom he had come to establish. Blessedness is not something we can obtain by our own efforts, but it is a gift bestowed by God on those open to the gift.

Matthew used the term, "Kingdom of Heaven," rather than "Kingdom of God" as Luke did, because he was writing for the Jewish community. The Jews had many titles for the Holy One, such as "Lord," but they looked upon the word, "Yahweh" which we translate "God," as the personal name of the Almighty.

It is difficult for us today to understand the close association, in the Jewish culture, of a name with the person. The name expressed the identity of the person. To know the name was to know the person. The Jews realized that they could never know fully the mystery of their Lord, so for several centuries before the time of Jesus, they had ceased to pronounce the sacred name. In deference to this tradition of the

Jewish community, Matthew wrote, "Kingdom of Heaven."

In our American culture, the word "Kingdom" has many negative connotations. The very thought of living in a kingdom is repugnant to many citizens of a democracy. Also, women are becoming more sensitive to words that imply male dominance as *king*dom does. So in order to really appreciate the Beatitudes, we need to understand what the word meant to Jesus and to the people who listened to him on the mountainside.

Jesus was expressing a very basic truth: God created the world and his right to rule over the world is unlimited. Jesus knew that he would have to clarify for his audience the true nature of God's Kingdom. The Jews responded enthusiastically to the word, "Kingdom," for they constantly looked for someone to free them from the hated Roman domination and re-establish their own kingdom. They hoped that Jesus would be the fulfillment of their hopes and dreams. Several times, Jesus was forced to flee because they desired to make him king and he knew how difficult it would be for them to accept his concept of kingdom. Most of the parables Jesus told about the Kingdom aimed at correcting this false interpretation of

God's reign and the mission of the Messiah.

A careful reading of the Kingdom parables and Jesus' interpretation of some of them reveals that Jesus was talking about the activity of God in the world. Having given human beings free will, God does not force goodness, love or blessings on anyone. So the Kingdom is like treasure in a field, or a pearl of great worth, that one must seek above all else. The Kingdom is like yeast, hidden in flour, which permeates and affects the entire mass. God's activity is experienced as initiatives or urges attracting human beings to greater truth, beauty, goodness and love. As these qualities are made visible in the world, God's presence becomes more evident to those with faith to see beyond outward appearances. So the Kingdom grows slowly like the mustard seed.

The paradox of the Kingdom is that it is already present in the world through God's activity but it is yet to come in all its fullness. The great privilege of human beings is that they can choose to cooperate with God's activity and help to bring the Kingdom to fulfillment.

Unfortunately some human actions and intentions hamper God's activity and retard the growth of the Kingdom. The disciples and followers of Jesus today are challenged to overcome these obstacles and allow God's activity to blossom ever more fully. This will be accomplished by a deeper awareness of the power of the Beatitudes and an enthusiastic, joyful commitment to Beatitude living.

This book is designed for individual or group use. It can be read, used for reflection and prayer by an individual. However, many people find a deeper, richer experience by sharing their reflections with a group. The prayer suggestions and discussion questions at the end of the book, provide the basis for group interaction and faith sharing.

THE BEATITUDES

"Blessed are the poor in spirit,
for theirs is the kingdom of heaven."
(Mt 5:3)

THE POOR IN SPIRIT

*M*any Christians find this first saying of Jesus
on the mountain the most challenging and the
most confusing of the Beatitudes. Besides the
words "blessed" and "kingdom" common to all
the Beatitudes and already considered in the
Introduction, a problem arises in trying to define *poor*.

If you were to ask an Arabian sheikh from
Dubai, a middle-class American, and an In-
dian living in the streets of Calcutta the meaning of poverty, what different interpretations
you would get! Each would define *poor* in terms
of a particular culture and its economic conditions. Poverty has little, if any, meaning in the
experience of citizens of oil-rich Arab
countries. Middle-class Americans are sometimes familiar with the poverty of others in their

own city. They also face the evidence of homelessness in large cities as they watch the evening news in their cozy living rooms. However, it is incomprehensible for most Americans that a quarter of a million Indians in Calcutta are born, live and die in the streets without ever having had even a shack to call home. How then, can a Christian make sense of this Beatitude and incorporate it in a meaningful way into the Christian life?

Reflection on the way the early Christian communities interpreted this first Beatitude can provide some leads. The first followers of Christ had to internalize his teachings. They brought to this process their Jewish heritage and the realities of living in a specific culture at a particular time in history. They struggled to express the values of Jesus, including the Beatitudes, in their society.

Each of the Evangelists wrote for a particular community and from a different perspective. And so we find slightly different versions of this Beatitude in Luke's and Matthew's Gospels. Luke recalled what Isaiah had written: that the arrival of the long-promised Messiah would bring blessings to the "little" people, the seemingly insignificant folk. So Luke wrote, "Blessed are you who are poor, the kingdom of God is yours" (Lk 6:20). According to Luke, Jesus announced to the materially poor, the hungry and dispossessed of his day, that they were the recipients of God's blessing.

How astounded Jesus' listeners must have been! Everyone knew that riches were a sign of God's favor and blessing. The story of Job provided a dramatic example of this belief. As a man of wealth, Job had the reputation of being in God's favor. When Job lost everything — his wealth, family, home, and even his health — his friends interpreted his misfortunes as a sign of his falling from favor with God. They could not believe that he had not offended God seriously and therefore was being punished by God.

But on the mountainside, Jesus said that the *poor* are the ones who are blessed by God. In one brief statement Jesus turned his listeners' world upside down. They were so accustomed to thinking of themselves as nothing and suddenly Jesus said that the poor are important to God! Their hearts were filled with incredulous joy! They asked themselves, "Who is this man?" He left them breathless but feeling an inner dignity for the first time in their lives.

However, when Matthew wrote his Gospel,

the Christian community included people who were not materially poor. Certainly the basic teaching of Jesus must be applicable to them too. After all, material poverty is not a good in itself. It is often a hindrance to full human living. A person can hardly be concerned about intellectual and spiritual things when every bit of energy is needed to obtain food and shelter. From this perspective, how might Matthew's community interpret this statement of Jesus?

The early Christian community realized it was not the mere lack of material possessions that opened a person's heart to God's reign. Rather, what Jesus saw in the poor around him, and what he shared with them, was a condition of mind and heart, an admission of dependence on God. To express this new insight, Matthew wrote: "Blessed are the *poor in spirit*" (Mt 5:3).

Perhaps the translation of this verse in *The New English Bible* is even better at getting to the core of Jesus' meaning, of opening a new way of thinking about this Beatitude. It reads: "How blest are those who know their need of God; the kingdom of Heaven is theirs."

Knowing one's need of God is acknowledging one's insufficiency, one's vulnerability. The person who is "poor in spirit" stands before God empty-handed, perhaps even aware that all is gift from God. This individual has a nonpossessive attitude that willingly shares God's gifts with others, realizing that the human person is worth more than any possession. It implies a nongrasping approach to life and a conscious sense of actually depending on God for life, truth, love and freedom. To illustrate this truth, Jesus told a parable:

> There was a rich man whose land produced a bountiful harvest. He asked himself, "What shall I do, for I do not have space to store my harvest?" And he said, "This is what I shall do. I shall tear down my barns and build larger ones. There I shall store all my grains and other goods, and I shall say to myself, 'Now as for you, you have so many good things stored up for many years, rest, eat, drink and be merry!' " But God said to him, "You fool, this night your life will be demanded of you and the things you have prepared, to whom will they belong?" (Lk 12:16-20)

In Jesus' time to call a person "fool" was a sign of great contempt. In this parable Jesus used this strong word to describe a man who put his trust in material things. This man was self-sufficient. He had wealth and depended on his riches for all that he needed in life.

The spirit of this first beatitude is contrary to the attitude of this puffed-up egotist. It is realizing that one's inner poverty cannot be satisfied by assets in the bank, social status or power over others. It is knowing in one's heart that all that the world holds is not enough. It is not a matter of wanting less in life but of seeking *more*. Looking at all God's gifts, one turns to God and says, "Thank you, God, for all your gifts. But I want more; I need *you*."

As Matthew and the early Jewish community interpreted the first Beatitude according to the signs of their times, Christians now need to re-interpret this statement of Jesus for today. This is not an easy task and can only be accomplished through the light and power of the Spirit.

In his first letter to the Corinthians, Paul tells us we must depend on the Spirit to develop a discerning attitude toward life if we are to live according to the values of Jesus: ". . . no one knows what pertains to God except the Spirit of God. We have not received the spirit of the world but the Spirit that is from God, so that we may understand the things freely given us by God" (1 Cor 2:11-12). Paul uses the phrase, "spirit of the world" to refer to values contrary to the values of Jesus.

We cannot escape the environment of false values in which we live, but we can learn to be critical of the things we see and hear — not in a negative, reactive spirit, but in a probing, testing way. Instead of accepting everything presented to us, we can make discriminating decisions on the basis of Jesus' values. We then take responsibility for our own lives instead of letting ourselves be dominated by ads and TV commercials which appeal to our wants rather than to our needs, and we are able to make responsible decisions that lead to a fuller life in the image of Jesus. The more one accumulates things and becomes engrossed in possessions, always striving for greater wealth, the more time one consumes in the care and maintenance of property and assets.

Besides creating false desires, TV commercials can influence us in another way. They can feed and increase our fears of danger from fire, flood, burglary, old age, sickness or disability. They promise security through the latest alarm system, improved locks, insurance — all those gadgets that only increase the fears they are meant to alleviate. They can lead us to place our security in something besides God. We can forget our need of God.

The lack of security has taken on a new meaning in a world where nuclear weapons can bring about total annihilation of the human race. It is absurd to put one's trust in anything that can disappear in a flash, be consumed in a cloud of radioactive dust. Knowing that God alone is enduring, that our true dignity lies in our relationship with God, we must acknowledge our need for God. All material things, even other people, are so fragile; it is obvious that our only solid security is God.

One of the joys of being poor in spirit is having time to enjoy people. Nonpossessiveness frees the heart to accept people. We begin to see others as they really are when we become less interested in the clothes they are wearing, the cars they are driving, or the neighborhood where they live. To begin to see the dignity of people is to recognize the bond that draws us all together as members of God's family. The awareness of this bond is the basis for a realization of the interdependence of all living things.

As Americans we like to think of ourselves as independent people. Since the writing of the Declaration of Independence, we have taken pride in our freedom, our initiative and our ability to get things done. We want to stand on our own two feet and not feel indebted to anyone or anything. This is the spirit that motivated the pioneers and continues to attract immigrants to this land of opportunity.

In spite of our love of independence, an honest evaluation of human existence reveals that in reality we are *not* independent. A truer statement of our human condition is "We are all interdependent." The spiritual basis for this interdependence is found in the very first book of Scripture.

God's revelation in Genesis begins with the image of God as creator. The two accounts of creation picture a tremendously generous God pouring forth an abundance of plant and animal life, filling the earth, air and sea with vibrant beauty. Surrounding the earth is the vast universe whose extent defies the imagination.

From a human perspective, the author of Genesis then wrote: "Since on the seventh day God was finished with the work he had been doing, he rested on the seventh day from all the work he had undertaken" (Gn 2:2). If one takes this statement literally, one might suppose that God is no longer active in creation. This supposition is far from the truth. God continues to create, even to this moment, for God continu-

11

ally pours creative energy into all living things, an energy that constantly ebbs and flows throughout the universe. It is this relationship with our Creator and the universal sharing of God's creative energy that is the spiritual basis for interdependence.

This interdependence is expressed so often in daily living that it is surprising that we ever think of ourselves as independent. Except in rare instances, food, clothing, housing, education, medical care, contact with society, protection from various dangers, etc. all reveal our interdependence with others. Life would be very different indeed if we each tried "to go it alone."

This web of interdependence extends, not only between all human beings, but between all creation. In recent years scientists in various fields have become fascinated by the concept of interdependence. Biologists, physicists, chemists, anthropologists and others, are discovering intimate links between the various elements of animate and inanimate creation. For example, John Storer, a biologist, claims that every square mile of soil on earth contains soil particles from every other square mile on earth. Or closer at hand, one has only to look at the weather report on the evening news to see a reminder of our interdependence. The air we breathe today in the Midwest filled the lungs of people in the far West several days ago. The scientist, Brian Swimme, maintains that each time we take in a deep breath we breathe some of the air that Jesus breathed.

Having so much in common, what a blessing it is that there are some differences to give diversity and richness to life. As we become more aware of our interdependence, such considerations as color, ethnic background, or financial status are no longer seen as differences that give rise to prejudice but diversity that enriches life.

Jesus tells us to ask and we shall receive. What more can we ask than a deep trust that tells God we know our need for him? Realizing our need of God changes the focus of our prayer. We begin to spend time asking God for an awareness of his presence in all the events of life. We desire to be more sensitive to God's action in life, to put more trust in God's loving care. God's unconditional love becomes real and we notice so many indications that we are not alone in life's struggles.

Trusting in God does not take away the hardships, the struggles and sufferings of life. But Jesus has guaranteed that the one who trusts in him lives now in the reign of God and will someday share the fullness of his Kingdom. Living in the Kingdom now gives the assurance that God is not only present in his creation, but he is active in history and in our individual lives. This conviction of God's presence and activity *now* gives an optimistic vision of life: No matter what is happening, God *can* and *does* bring some good out of it. There is hope for the future because the future does not depend on human beings alone.

Having this vision of life reduces the fears, tensions, and worries that are all a part of daily living and brings the promised reward of this Beatitude. "The Kingdom of God is yours" (Lk 6:20). Jesus used the present tense in expressing the rewards of this Beatitude. One does not have to wait for the future fulfillment of the Kingdom to be blessed. If you are poor in spirit, Jesus says you are blessed NOW.

"Blessed are they who mourn,
for they shall be comforted."
(Mt 5:4)

THE SORROWFUL

*I*n the second Beatitude, Jesus again startled his audience and all future disciples: "Blessed are they who mourn"! The *sorrowful* are blessed? No matter how we understand sorrow, we just do not like it. How could Jesus possibly say that we are blessed when we weep?

The human foundation for the second Beatitude is a recognition of all our emotions. A brief look at the place of emotions in human life can make this Beatitude more meaningful.

God made us emotional beings. God gifts us with emotions to enrich our lives and increase our potential for greater happiness. Emotions, in themselves, are morally neutral, neither good nor bad. They arise spontaneously and only then can we decide how we will handle them. Through our response, feelings can be used to deepen our relationship with God or mar that relationship.

Unfortunately, we tend to label emotions in positive or negative terms. We *like* to feel affection or love for another so we call this emotion "good." Anger may make us uncomfortable so we label it "bad." While we may hesitate to call sadness, sorrow, or grief "bad," we frequently think of these emotions as negative. However, incidents in the life of Jesus teach us to accept *all* our emotions as part of our humanity.

John recorded one such incident as happening very early in the public life of Jesus. It indicates vividly how Jesus expressed his emotions.

> Since the Passover of the Jews was near, Jesus went up to Jerusalem. He found in the temple area those who sold oxen, sheep, and doves, as well as the money-changers seated there. He made a whip out of cords and drove them all out of the temple area, with the sheep and oxen, and spilled the coins of the money-changers and overturned their tables, and to those who sold doves he said, "Take these out of here, and stop making my Father's house a marketplace." (Jn 3:13-16)

Jesus was *really* angry but his anger was not out of control. The sellers of doves were poorer than the other merchants in the temple precincts. They provided doves for the poor to offer in sacrifice so Jesus treated them more gently. He did not overturn their tables or scatter their coins but expressed his anger in words.

Being in touch with one's emotions does not imply always expressing them outwardly, for some expressions of feelings can be destructive. It is necessary to recognize and accept the feelings that are present and then decide an appropriate way to handle them. For example, if I am very angry at someone, I can admit my anger, at least to myself. Then I must make a choice. Will I lash out at the next person who crosses my path, or will I do something constructive to release my energy and later resolve the situation in a responsible way?

Another incident recorded by John occurred shortly before Jesus' passion and death. Some Scripture scholars point out that this event — the raising of Lazarus from the dead — convinced the Jewish rulers that they must lose no time in apprehending Jesus.

Martha met Jesus outside Bethany and

then hurried to inform her sister, Mary, that
Jesus was asking for her.

> When Mary came to where Jesus was and
> saw him, she fell at his feet and said to
> him, "Lord, if you had been here, my
> brother would not have died." When
> Jesus saw her weeping and the Jews who
> had come with her weeping, he became
> perturbed and deeply troubled, and said,
> "Where have you laid him?" They said to
> him, "Sir, come and see." And Jesus
> wept. (Jn 11:32-35)

In both these incidents, Jesus' response is
very different from the denial and repression
that can sometimes pass as calm and control.
The message we receive from modern society is
to escape, as much as possible, from any sadness, grief or even any pain or distress. If we
are at all realistic we realize how impossible
this is.

If we cannot escape the events that cause
mourning, then we are told, "At least *try* to
pretend this did not happen." Sometimes fans
of movie stars or popular singers continue to
deny their idols' death and claim to see them in
all kinds of unlikely places.

More generally, people try in many ways to

avoid facing the death of a loved one. The mortician is praised for his ability to make the corpse look alive and merely sleeping. "How beautiful and natural she looks!" friends remark to the grieving relatives.

In spite of psychologists' warnings that unexpressed grief can cause much emotional and physical harm, expressions of grief are not acceptable in polite society. Often we are uncomfortable even witnessing on TV the public wailing, so common in Eastern cultures, as an expression of grief.

Often adults try to shield children from the reality of death by maintaining a cheerful front. They make strenuous efforts not to cry in the presence of the children. Thus, the children are given the unspoken message that it is not acceptable to cry. They are not given permission to grieve and express their sorrow but are taught to repress their feelings.

Psychologists have discovered that when tears are shed in sorrow or distress, chemicals such as adrenaline, various hormones and endorphin, a pain reliever, are released. Through this release, tensions are discharged and calm and balance restored. Tears caused by irritants, such as dust or pollen, do not have this healing effect.

In an imperfect world every person knows times of sadness and trouble. We cannot entirely escape this reality of our human condition. The crucial question is, how do we handle these times? Since we cannot escape and only harm ourselves by pretense, then it seems that the only alternative is to accept the emotions associated with suffering and sorrow.

It is important to distinguish true acceptance from self-pity. Rose Kennedy was preparing to go to Mass when she heard the announcement of Robert's assassination on the radio. She might have collapsed in self-pity at the violent death of a second son but instead she continued on her way to Mass to pray for him.

To acknowledge one's feelings of sorrow is very different from wallowing in that sorrow, pitying oneself for feeling this way and demanding that others recognize how much one is suffering. Acceptance, on a natural level, is admitting, "Yes, I am sorrowful and I weep in my grief."

Spiritually, acceptance recognizes how sorrow and other human afflictions are a part of human reality. One does not blame God, as God does not inflict suffering on human beings. Much unnecessary turmoil and distress can be avoided by a clearer understanding of the relationship of God to physical and emotional suffering.

God wants us to be happy and does not inflict suffering and sorrow. Neither does God stand aloof from our sorrow. Because of the presence of sin in the world we are all born into a flawed world. We enter into the human condition that is limited and not perfect and by our personal failures and sins we contribute to the condition that affects every human being. So together, we struggle all our lives with various physical weaknesses, and emotional and psychological limitations.

Where is God in all our struggles? God loves us with an unconditional love and is always present to give us the support and consolation we need, if we but ask. In time of great sorrow, we need to move beyond the spontaneous question, "Why me, Lord?" to the simple request, "Help me, God," trusting that is just what God wants to do. Jesus does *not* tell us to make our own consolation as friends sometimes do when they say, "Cheer up!" Jesus urges us to be open to receiving the consolation that he will give us.

We should not approach the sorrowful, the troubled, the depressed in order to give advice or material help while remaining outside their suffering. The spirit of the Beatitude challenges us to enter with them into the sorrow, the trouble, the depression. It demands recognizing our inability to take away the sorrow and being willing to be *with* others *in* their pain.

Living this Beatitude at times requires great patience and a nonjudgmental attitude. If a person seems to continue grieving longer than we think is reasonable or healthy, we may be tempted to say, "That's enough! Get on with life!" The sorrowing person may want very much to get on with life but still remains "stuck" in sorrow. For the grief-stricken, a sense of paralysis seems to make action impossible.

We tend to think of sorrow and grief in terms of the death of a loved one. If we look at the sense of loss experienced at this time we realize that there are other tragedies in life that have the same psychological effect.

Psychiatrists, psychologists and marriage counselors note that the trauma of divorce is often similar to the shock which follows the death of a close friend or relative. There is the same sense of loss, the same feeling of living in an unreal world, the feeling that one will soon wake up and find the event a bad dream.

Divorce, as well as death, gives rise to anger that one's life has been drastically changed and to a desire to lash out against the person perceived as causing the change. Grief too is often mixed with anger, depression and guilt. The grieving process then needs to include reconciliation and self-forgiveness if consolation is to follow.

Jesus told his disciples that his heart was moved to pity by the poor (Mk 6:34). He understood them and saw that they were even robbed of energy and initiative to help themselves. They needed someone to bring them consolation.

We too see a whole segment of our society whose lives are characterized by a pervading sorrow. Living in continual poverty fills the soul with paralyzing sadness. The poor are often criticized for apathy and laziness. Those who work with them frequently meet frustration when people fail to respond to efforts to assist them in bettering their condition. Deeper than the fear of reprisal lies the paralysis imposed by the loss of their dignity and self-esteem.

As in other incidents of loss, the poor must be allowed to grieve before they are free to act.

They must be provided with opportunities to express their deep sorrow so they are no longer immobilized. They must be encouraged to tell their stories to listening hearts who will grieve with them. This can be a long, slow process that seems unending. What a wealth of patience and empathy must precede the coming of the consolation Jesus has promised!

By sharing in the mission of Jesus we can help to comfort the sorrowful. Jesus explained his mission to the people of Nazareth by applying the words of Isaiah to himself. Standing in their midst, he read from the scroll presented to him:

> "The Spirit of the Lord is upon me, because he has anointed me to bring glad tidings to the poor. He has sent me to proclaim liberty to captives and recovery of sight to the blind, and to let the oppressed go free, and to proclaim a year acceptable to the Lord." (Lk 4:18-19)

Isaiah mentioned those he saw around him in special need of God's comfort. Disciples of Jesus today see the homeless, abused women and children, those with AIDS or other terminal illnesses, and the elderly — all mourning and sorrowing. God has promised to comfort them. They begin to experience God's consolation through the gentle touch and the soothing voice of a compassionate, caring person who is with them in their suffering.

A prayerful reading of the Gospels reveals how the radical message of Jesus in the Beatitudes was personified in his own life. The first two Beatitudes came together in such a profound way in Jesus' agony in the garden. In his extreme distress Jesus turned to his Father. He put his complete trust in the Father's will, knowing that the Father would give him the strength to complete his mission. He had come to preach the Kingdom and, for Jesus, the Kingdom was in his Father's will. When we know our need of God the Kingdom becomes present in our lives too.

Jesus looked to his chosen friends to be with him in his sorrow. What a unique opportunity these apostles had to live the second Beatitude! Leaving Jesus alone in his sorrow, how could they share in the consolation given him by the Father? Jesus found strength to go forth to meet his victorious death and new life. He awakened his apostles and said, "Up, let us go forward . . ." (Mt 26:46). Here we see the pattern of the second Beatitude. Entering into the sorrows of life, we too are strengthened so that we can get up and be on our way to new life.

*"Blessed are the meek,
for they will inherit the land."*
(Mt 5:5)

THE GENTLE

*O*n that sunny day in Galilee, Jesus looked at the crowd gathered around him. He had just announced to them that those who know their need of God are already experiencing the Kingdom. He had proclaimed to them that those who are sorrowful will be consoled. How would they receive the rest of his message?

Jesus knew these people well. He knew how much their ancestors had suffered at the hands of more powerful nations. He realized how they chafed under the yoke of Rome and how they longed for the opportunity to fight for their freedom. They were always looking for the one who would lead them to victory over Rome. Over the years they had come to identify this hoped-for leader with the Messiah promised by God through the prophets.

Would Jesus dare to tell them that the meek, not the violent, would inherit the land? No matter how radical it sounded, he must pass on to them the message of the Kingdom he had come to preach. As always, Jesus was faithful to his mission. He proclaimed for all to hear that the earth would fall to the gentle-hearted.

What did the people of Jesus' time think about such a message? What do we think of it?

The Jews of Jesus' time were perhaps more open to a call to gentleness than we are. They were steeped in Old Testament spirituality. They knew how often meekness had been mentioned in the Psalms. Perhaps they thought specifically of Psalm 37:

> Do not strive to outdo the evildoers
> or emulate those who do wrong.
> For like the grass they soon wither,
> and fade like the green of spring.
> (Ps 37:1-2)

In a subsequent verse the psalmist elaborates:

> But the humble shall possess the land
> and enjoy untold prosperity.
> (Ps 37:11)

Listening to Jesus, the people may have recalled the many times in their history when God had been their liberator. God had saved them from powerful enemies when they turned to him in trust and repentance. Perhaps they heard the message of Jesus as a continuation of the saving action of their God. Jesus was saying to them, "There is no need for you to hate the wicked, to react with violence, for God will save you as he has done so often in the past."

Meekness stands in the middle between extreme rage and complete absence of anger. We should not make the mistake of thinking that the person of gentle spirit never gets angry. A careful reading of the Gospels reveals times when Jesus was angry. He was angry with the Scribes and Pharisees when they misled the people (Lk 11:52). He overturned the tables of the money changers who were profaning the house of God (Mk 11:15-18). Note that Jesus grew angry at those who oppressed the powerless and the poor, never because he himself was suffering injustice.

Jesus gave us a perfect example of meekness as he stood before the high priest:

The high priest questioned Jesus about his disciples and about his doctrine.

Jesus answered him, "I have spoken publicly to the world. I have always taught in a synagogue or in the temple area, where all the Jews gather, and in secret I have said nothing. Why ask me? Ask those who heard me what I said to them. They know what I said." When he had said this, one of the temple guards standing there struck Jesus and said, "Is this the way you answer the high priest?" Jesus answered him, "If I have spoken wrongly, testify to the wrong; but if I have spoken rightly, why do you strike me?"

(Jn 18:19-23)

Jesus had the courage to answer openly, but did not allow the high priest to put him on the defensive about his teachings. When he was slapped, Jesus replied to the injustice in a nonviolent way.

Reflecting on the relationship between anger and meekness, we might say that meekness controls anger and expresses it in ways which are appropriate, proportionate and never destructive. It is the strength to resist reacting violently when under attack. It is choosing in true freedom a nonviolent response to a difficult situation.

Meekness is not apathy, nor is it the passivity that accepts injustice. Rather it implies the inner strength to take nonviolent action even in the face of great injustice. There is a power in meekness that the violent cannot understand.

An incident in the life of Gandhi illustrates the strength of meekness. Although not a Christian, Gandhi was convinced of the truth of this Beatitude. One day as he led the Indians in a demonstration against the unfair salt laws, the British soldiers began clubbing the first line of protesters. Immediately, others took their place, and suffered the same fate. They were replaced by another group. On and on the Indians came. Finally, the British soldiers had to turn away. Their own humanity would not allow them to continue their violence in the face of such inner strength. The meek Indians were victorious.

What is Jesus saying to us today in this third Beatitude? He is *still* saying that we are blessed if we are meek and gentle. The message has not changed. The question is, how do we hear it? What does it mean in our lives?

If we find this third Beatitude hard to accept, there may be some consolation in knowing that the disciples too found meekness difficult. One time they came to Jesus with the question, "Who is the greatest in the kingdom of heaven?" Jesus answered their question by putting a child in their midst and saying: "Amen, I say to you, unless you turn and become like children, you will not enter the kingdom of heaven. Whoever humbles himself as this child is the greatest in the kingdom of heaven" (Mt 18:1-4).

The spontaneity, the vulnerability and the loving tenderness of a child are all qualities of a gentle heart. These qualities that come so naturally to a child need a gentle home atmosphere in which to develop and mature.

Parents who see meekness as an important value for their children have many obstacles to overcome. Our society does not value meekness. TV programs are filled with all forms of violent behavior. Violence is made to seem exciting, clever and very much a part of the lives of attractive people. Children are provided with "toys" that help them mimic the violence they see on TV. Even watching the evening news, one has the impression that people all over the world are fighting each other. Having surrounded children with violence, how can the American public be shocked when a six-year-old shoots his ten-year-old brother?

Unfortunately, some children are further harmed by witnessing and experiencing violence among family members. Wife and child abuse are becoming more prevalent. Various studies show that violence in the home is self-perpetuating. A boy who has an abusive father, whose mother is the victim of violence in the home, frequently becomes an abusive husband and father himself.

Frustration and stress are inevitable in our society, so it is essential for families to work out ways to relieve tension in a nonviolent way. Open communication is essential to a harmonious family life. If members of the family can be honest in revealing to one another those trivial annoyances that add to tension in daily life, they can defuse situations that might trigger anger and violence. It takes the cooperation of both parents and children to make the home a loving place.

This Beatitude is not easy and most of us will fail over and over again, just as the apostles did. At the Last Supper Jesus had just given himself to the apostles as their nourishment and strength. Even in this atmosphere of complete self-giving, the apostles began arguing *again* about who would be the greatest (Lk 22:24).

Two thousand years later this competitive spirit is still so prevalent in our United States culture that meekness seems very un-American. We are noted for our free enterprise system, for those qualities which ensure that an individual will get ahead in life. The competitive spirit and, even more, a ruthless aggressiveness seem to be the foundation for success in the business world. Climbing the ladder of success often means stepping on those who get in the way.

Does meekness then condemn a person to failure in the business world? Meekness neither condemns to failure nor does it guarantee success. Rather, it indicates the inner attitude that should be present as a goal is pursued. It is the nonviolent way of moving toward a goal, using authentically human means that do not harm others.

The third Beatitude promises that the meek will inherit the land. The earth belongs to God but God will share it with the people of the Kingdom. When something belongs to us we cherish it and want to protect it. We try to keep it in good condition and see to it that others do not mar its beauty. If we think of the earth as our temporary possession then we will treat it with reverence and respect.

Possession of the earth, however, may not be individualistic or exclusive. *All* those of gentle heart inherit the earth. It is a community possession for the good of all. Those who consider the earth their own individual possession to be used and abused without consideration of others are not living in the promise of this Beatitude. They are contradicting the gentle spirit that is the basis for the promise.

The gentle cultivate the earth; they treat all living things as God's creatures. They use the resources of the earth sparingly, knowing that the supply is limited. They delight in the abundance our Father shares with us. As they replace violence and excessive competitiveness with gentleness, creation too is set free.

The Jews listening to Jesus heard this promise in the context of their history. They had been a nomadic people and God had made a covenant with them. God promised to lead them into a land flowing with milk and honey. The Promised Land was filled with everything the Israelites needed to lead a happy, prosperous life. They were to enjoy the Promised Land as long as they remembered God and did not become haughty. The beautiful, rich land God promised to the Israelites is symbolic of the

Kingdom whose fullness Jesus promises in this Beatitude.

Our land too is symbolic of the Kingdom fulfilled. The abundance and variety of living things are all reminders of the richness we will share in the future Kingdom. The promise of this future Kingdom depends on learning from Jesus to be gentle and humble of heart. We anticipate, Paul tells us, "things beyond our seeing, things beyond our hearing, things beyond our imagining, all prepared by God" (1 Cor 2:9).

"Blessed are they who
hunger and thirst for righteousness,
for they will be satisfied."
(Mt 5:6)

THE JUST

*T*he word "righteousness" is a Biblical term
found frequently in the Jewish Scriptures and
several times in Matthew's Gospel. Matthew's
first use of the word occurs in his description of
Joseph as a "righteous" man, that is a man
devoted to the observance of the Mosaic law.
More generally, righteousness is understood as
moral conformity to God's will.

However, when the word is used again in
Chapter 3 it has a slightly different meaning:

Then Jesus came from Galilee to John at
the Jordan to be baptized by him. John
tried to prevent him, saying, "I need to be
baptized by you, and yet you are coming
to me?" Jesus said to him in reply, "Allow
it now, for thus it is fitting for us to fulfill
all righteousness." (Mt 3:13-15)

"To fulfill" usually refers to the fulfillment of prophecy, understanding prophecy as the recounting of the saving action of God. It seems that Jesus was telling John that it was important for the fulfillment of God's saving action that the Messiah be identified with sinners. The affirmation of the voice from heaven, saying, "This is my beloved Son, with whom I am well pleased," (Mt 3:17) seems to support this interpretation.

When righteousness is used in the fourth Beatitude it again seems to mean the saving activity of God. What does it mean to "hunger and thirst for the saving activity of God"?

Jesus spoke this Beatitude to poor people living in a dry, sandy land. Hunger and thirst were experiences of daily living. They knew what it meant to feel the pangs of hunger, to experience dry, parched throats. Hunger and thirst connote the absence of something necessary as well as the intense desire to bring about a state of harmony and balance to the body that feels deprived. They also knew that God intended that these appetites be satisfied, for he had fed their ancestors in the desert and promised them a land overflowing with milk and honey.

Jesus used this experience of natural

hunger and thirst to help the people understand a deeper, spiritual craving. He told them
that just as our bodies crave food and drink, so
our hearts should crave God's saving activity.

What is this divine dynamism that Jesus
wants us to crave with the intensity of a starving
person? Or put in another way, what does God
want to accomplish in the world?

We might get a hint by using another translation of the Bible which states this Beatitude:
"Blessed are they who hunger and thirst for
justice. . . ." Basically justice means having
available for all people what is necessary to
become fully human in the image of Jesus.

This Beatitude challenges us to desire
wholeheartedly to become fully human
ourselves and to help others do the same. Our
desire for justice should be experienced as a
fierce craving — not a feeling that justice
would be nice, but a craving that demands to
be satisfied.

Hunger and thirst deeply experienced
banish apathy. The person makes every effort,
no matter how weak, to overcome the lack. Our
craving for justice should likewise lead to action that will bring about a state of inner
harmony and outward peace. This action is
aimed at removing two kinds of obstacles: both

the hindrances within ourselves and oppression from without which prevent us from reaching our true potential. The temptation is to attack the outward oppressions while being oblivious to the inner bondage.

We can be so blind to the barriers that hinder our growth in the image of Jesus. We need to follow the example of the blind beggar on the road near Jericho. He heard the crowd approaching and learning that Jesus was near, he cried out, "Jesus, son of David, have pity on me." Even when the crowd rebuked him, he continued to call out, "Son of David, have pity on me." When Jesus asked him, "What do you want me to do for you?" the blind man answered, "Master, I want to see" (Mk 11:46-50).

Jesus never fails to answer a desire for light made with the humble recognition of one's need of God. The result of this sincere prayer is the heightening of one's spiritual awareness of these inner obstacles. A little reflection reveals that our own sinfulness hampers our growth toward full humanity.

This sinfulness is more than the sinful acts of commission or omission of which we are conscious. We all share a rootedness in evil that goes deeper than individual acts, deeper than we alone have the power to effect. We need God's saving action. Only then can we begin to turn our lives around. Traditionally this process has been called "conversion." Today many people call this experience "being born again." However we describe this experience, it involves being turned in a new direction. We move away from the false values that entrap us toward the values of Jesus that give us freedom.

But this is only the first step to living in the spirit of this Beatitude. In the time of Isaiah, widows and orphans had no way of obtaining the necessities of life. God made it clear through his prophet, Isaiah, that in the face of this injustice he (God) expected more from the people than lifting up their hands in prayer. God says:

> When you spread your hands,
>   I close my eyes to you;
> Though you pray the more,
>   I will not listen. . . .

Put away your misdeeds from before my eyes;
    cease doing evil; learn to do good.
Make justice your aim: redress the wronged,
    hear the orphan's plea, defend the widow.
Come now, let us set things right,
    says the Lord.   (Is 1:15-18a)

41

God said, "let *us* set things right." Justice, or setting "things right," is a cooperative effort of God and human beings. When people intensely crave justice and make strenuous efforts to bring it about, then God's saving action can make those efforts effective.

Today, as we look beyond our own need for inner conversion, we see that many oppressive conditions in society interfere with the growth of human beings to their full potential. We see that some people cannot develop physically, psychologically or spiritually because they are forced to live in inhuman conditions. Lack of nourishing food, decent housing, adequate medical care and a solid education are conditions which keep many people in virtual slavery.

It is the work of justice to fight against these oppressions. Justice struggles to make it possible for everyone to work for a wage that ensures the necessities of decent human living. The standard for a decent human life may vary from one culture to another, but the basics of food, clothing, decent housing, medical care and education should be available to all people.

No one says that working for justice is easy. It involves much more than giving Christmas baskets to needy families; that is a work of charity. Justice aims at changing the very *structures* in society that keep people impoverished. The term "structures" denotes any law or any organizational way of doing things that discriminates against some group of people: the poor, people of a certain race or nationality, women. For example, a rich person who is suspected of committing a crime can post bond and be free until the case comes to court. A poor man who does not have money for the bond spends the time in jail. The very system that is supposed to work justice for all discriminates against him because of his poverty. He forfeits his freedom not because he is guilty of a crime but because he is poor. This is just one way the poor are treated unjustly in the richest country in the world.

Nearly all women who work outside the home suffer from sex discrimination. Until rather recently, many types of employment were not open to women. Even now, with greater freedom to choose their work, on an average, women are paid only about two-thirds the salary men make for the same work. These are only two examples of the way structures in our society work injustice against large numbers of people. In struggling for justice we try to change these structures.

Even mentioning the necessity to change "oppressive structures" can paralyze some people. As a person becomes more aware of injustice and feels called to respond, the challenge seems so great and individual efforts so puny! It seems that our only hope of success is to join with others who have the same goal. Paul tells us that it is the Spirit who draws these individuals together, not merely a common bond of human interest. Through the power of the Spirit, a community is formed which has more strength than the combined strength of the individuals forming it. Each receives strength, encouragement and new hope from the other members of the community and can begin to see possibilities for action that will have some effect on the oppressive structures (Ep 4:1-6, 16).

When Jesus talked to the crowds that followed him, he often used parables to clarify his message. He spoke of simple, homey things familiar to the people — a lamp, yeast in dough, a precious pearl, mustard seed, planting and harvesting crops.

One day Jesus told a parable about a farmer sowing seed. As the sower scattered the seed some fell on the path, some on rocky ground, some among thorns but some fell on good, rich soil (Mt 13:4-9). The disciples had difficulty understanding this parable until Jesus made it clear that the quality of the soil symbolized the way different people hear the Good News. If the message is heard and taken in, then it produces the fruit Jesus desires. Those who have heard the message of this Beatitude will produce action for justice. Where to begin?

One might start by studying legislation before Congress in light of its effect on the needy. A good factual letter stating your opinion can be very effective. Passing on your knowledge to others multiplies your effectiveness. In this way ordinary people can influence the legislators who make decisions about other's lives. This is a nonviolent way to change unjust structures.

Once a person becomes involved in working for justice, opportunities mushroom. The temptation is to be carried away by enthusiasm and try to do too much. The result is burnout, a state of exhaustion, frustration and despondency leading to the paralysis of inaction.

If our hunger and thirst for justice leads to action with others, then we will experience some satisfaction. At times we may feel overwhelmed by the depth and wide extent of the injustice in the world and see our best efforts resulting in so little progress. Then, more than ever, we need solid faith in the saving activity of God at work in the world, bringing about results we never dreamed were possible. It is satisfying to know that with God we can make a difference. Our complete satisfaction will come when the Kingdom is fulfilled.

"Blessed are the merciful,
for they will be shown mercy."
(Mt 5:7)

THE MERCIFUL

*J*esus intended all the Beatitudes taken together as a summary or pattern of Christian
living. By picking and choosing which
Beatitudes seem most congenial, the Christian
would risk an unbalanced life, at best. There is
a special risk for those who most enthusiastically hunger and thirst for justice. In their zeal
they may become harsh and judgmental of
those who do not see things their way. They
lose sight of the fact that we are all sinful and
weak.

Jesus pointed out this risk to his disciples
in a parable about two men who went to the
temple to pray. One was a Pharisee and the
other a tax collector. Pharisees and tax collectors were two groups of people well known to
Jesus' audience. The Pharisees prided

themselves on their fidelity to the smallest prescriptions of the law of Moses. They were pious, devoted Jews keeping alive their traditions even when dominated by a foreign power. They were admired by the simple people. However, the righteous Pharisees despised the publicans for collecting taxes for their Roman oppressors. The tax collectors were looked upon as traitors by their own people because they collaborated with the hated Romans.

Once again Jesus showed his disciples that his values were so different from the values of their world. He said:

> The Pharisee took up his position and spoke this prayer to himself: "O God, I thank you that I am not like the rest of humanity — greedy, dishonest, adulterous — or even like this tax collector. I fast twice a week, and I pay tithes on my income." But the tax collector stood off at a distance and would not even raise his eyes to heaven but beat his breast and prayed: "O God, be merciful to me a sinner." I tell you, the latter went home justified, not the former. (Lk 18:11-14a)

Keeping in mind this parable, one might suppose that Jesus stated the Beatitude,

"Blessed are the merciful," next as a balance. As we earnestly strive for greater justice in the world, justice must be tempered by a merciful heart. Even as we struggle for justice, we need to love and forgive those who are perpetrating injustice. Mercy focuses on concern for the wrongdoer as justice works to right the wrong being done.

It is difficult, if not impossible, to be merciful without first knowing one's own need for mercy from God. As members of God's family our actions have an effect for good or evil on our brothers and sisters. Looking within our own hearts and discovering our sinfulness, we feel helpless to break free. It is from such a sense of helplessness in the face of sin that one calls out to God for mercy. God's love is never deaf to such a call. We know from the parable that God responds to our prayer with his merciful forgiveness. Only then is it possible to be compassionate with the weakness of others.

Having had this experience of mercy, the one who hears the message of Jesus desires also to respond to human weakness with forgiving love. This is not being "soft," but learning to be compassionate in the way that God is compassionate. Instead of giving an abstract, theoretical explanation of the way to really live this Beatitude, Jesus told a story, as he so often did, to instruct his disciples.

One day a scholar of the law asked Jesus some subtle questions. In answer to the man's question, "Who is my neighbor?" Jesus told the parable of the traveler on the way from Jerusalem to Jericho. Along the way, the unfortunate wayfarer was robbed, beaten and left by the side of the road to die. Two Jews, a priest and a Levite, saw the man, but ignored his suffering and continued on their journey. Finally, a Samaritan picked him up, took him to an inn and cared for his wounds (Lk 10:29-35).

Samaritans were the descendants of Israelites who had intermarried with Assyrians. There was such hostility between the Samaritans and the Jews that many Jews would not pass through Samaria on journeys from Galilee to Judea. Since the traveler began his journey in Jerusalem, the implication is that he was a Jew. How difficult it must have been for the disciples to accept what Jesus was saying: a *Samaritan* helping a *Jew*!

The Samaritan does not question why this man is lying injured by the side of the road. He does not inquire into the man's past; he is not concerned whether the injured man is a good person or not, or whether he has the same religious beliefs or political convictions. The Samaritan sees only one thing: Here is a person in misery who needs his help. And he gives it generously.

When Jesus finished the story, he asked the scholar for his conclusion: "Which of these three, in your opinion, was neighbor to the robber's victim?" Apparently the scholar was a man of integrity, for he answered, "The one who treated him with mercy" (Lk 10:36-37).

Realizing that mercy reveals so clearly the action of God in a person's life that it has been called a "peculiarly Christian virtue," we might find it difficult to believe in the goodness and mercy of a non-Christian. Then is the time to put aside prejudice and admit that God's ways often do not fit human expectations.

On the evening of his Resurrection, Jesus *showed* vividly by his actions and attitudes the meaning of this Beatitude. We read in the Gospel of John:

On the evening of that first day of the week, when the doors were locked where the disciples were, for fear of the Jews, Jesus came and stood in their midst and said to them, "Peace be with you." When he had said this, he showed them his hands and his side. The disciples rejoiced when they saw the Lord. Jesus said to them again, "Peace be with you. As the Father has sent me, so I send you." And when he had said this, he breathed on them and said to them, "Receive the Holy Spirit. Whose sins you forgive are forgiven them, and whose sins you retain are retained. (Jn 20:19-23)

Notably, John uses the word *disciples* twice in this passage. The word *disciples* is a scriptural term meaning "learners" and was often used to denote those who followed Jesus and listened to his message. Therefore, it seems likely that others besides the apostles, the chosen twelve, were present behind the locked doors when Jesus appeared in their midst.

To the friends who had deserted him in his hour of need, Jesus' message was "Peace." They had been cowardly and weak but now their hearts were grieving for Jesus. He came to bring them his loving forgiveness. He did not accuse them or remind them of their failure to be with him when he needed their faithfulness. In one word, "Peace," he put all that in the past.

To show his total forgiveness, he sent them out to continue his work, to spread the Good News and be merciful to others. He picked them up out of their sadness and, in his merciful love, gave them the strength and confidence they needed to bring his message to others.

Jesus told his disciples, "Receive the Holy Spirit," for only in the power of his Spirit will his followers be able to forgive as he has done. Traditionally this passage has been associated with the Sacrament of Reconciliation. Seen in this context alone, we can fail to feel the demands Jesus is making on all his disciples.

We do not go far in life without being hurt, ignored or insulted by someone, whether deliberately or unintentionally. To be part of the Kingdom and live out this Beatitude is to accept the fact that "binding and loosing" are realities of our lives beyond our experience of the sacrament. Each time there are cutting words, insensitive actions or hostile feelings between two people this dynamic is operative. Either they release each other from the bond of sinfulness or they are both, in a sense, held bound. Unless they free each other, an unloving relationship harms both individuals and the community. The loving energy that should flow from their relationship is restricted. It is

53

bound and the whole Body is deprived.

Some Christians feel they are going far enough by saying, "I'll forgive that person; all she/he has to do is to apologize." This may sound forgiving, but it is also self-righteous. The blame is subtly put on the other person for the impasse; the other is expected to take the first step.

In order for the bonds to be broken it is often necessary for the *injured* person to take the first step. This first step is not only forgiveness in the heart, but a reaching out to the other with the mercy of Jesus. It is letting the other know that he or she is no longer being held bound. It is being able to say the Our Father with sincerity: "Forgive us our debts, *as we forgive* our debtors" (Mt 6:12).

As the disciples heard Jesus teach about forgiveness, a very natural question came to their minds. As usual it was Peter who voiced the question: "Lord, if my brother sins against me, how often must I forgive him? As many as seven times?" Apparently, Peter thought he was being generous in forgiving seven times. Like Peter we may think that forgiving seven times should be enough. But Jesus answered, "I say to you, not seven times but seventy-seven times" (Mt 18:21-22). By using such a large number, Jesus really said we should never stop forgiving.

As we too listen to Jesus telling us we must continue to forgive, it is important to distinguish between *forgiving* and *forgetting*. Some very sincere people are distressed to find that hurts they have truly tried to forgive in the past sometimes pop back into their consciousness. They see a person who has hurt them and suddenly the hurt is alive again, bringing with it feelings of anger and resentment. At such moments it is easy to doubt one's merciful heart and feel very guilty.

Everything that ever happened in our lives is still with us. Many memories lie buried in our unconscious. At times it takes very little to trigger a memory and release it to consciousness. With it comes all the emotional overtones with which it was associated. Instead of feeling guilty, this is an opportunity to renew forgiveness.

It is consoling to know that as the years pass memories often lose their power to disturb the heart. The important thing is not to become depressed when a memory surfaces, even when it is still packed with negative emotions. It is an opportunity to recognize our human limitations and to grasp again the opportunity to lift a person to the Lord in merciful, forgiving love. Each time we renew forgiveness for a past hurt, we are blessed for Jesus promised, "Blessed are the merciful, for they will be shown mercy" (Mt 5:7).

"Blessed are the clean of heart,
for they will see God."
(Mt 5:8)

THE PURE OF HEART

*M*any translations of this Beatitude read,
"Blessed are the pure of heart," and we readily
give assent to this message. Of all the
Beatitudes, we believe that *here* we know what
Jesus was saying and how it applies to our
lives. To anyone raised in a Christian home, it
seemed obvious that Jesus was talking about
those who faithfully observe the sixth and ninth
commandments. There was a time when the
notion of sinfulness was so focused on sins
against purity that anyone who kept at least
those two commandments was considered to be
on the highway to heaven.

However, this Beatitude, like the five already considered, is an ideal which encompas-
ses all of life and requires a much broader
understanding of the word *pure*. In ordinary

conversation when we say a substance is pure, we mean that it is everything it is meant to be. Other substances that might lessen its quality are absent. *Pure* implies that it is not adulterated by any harmful, inferior ingredients or even anything that might enhance its color, taste or texture.

Now as we take a closer look at the phrase "whose hearts are clean, or pure," we realize that the message of Jesus goes much deeper and is much more demanding than the sixth and ninth commandments.

A passage in Proverbs gives us a clearer understanding of the meaning of "heart" as used by Jesus and heard by his audience. The author wrote:

> My son, to my words be attentive,
>   to my sayings incline your ear;
> Let them not slip out of your sight,
>   keep them within your heart;
> For they are life to those who find them,
>   to man's whole being they are health.
> With closest custody, guard your heart,
>   for in it are the sources of life.
>   (Pr 4:20-24)

In this context, as Jesus proclaimed, "Blessed are the clean of heart," his listeners understood that living this Beatitude would affect their whole lives.

The Jews thought of the heart as the source of life, the center of thought and will. In other words, the heart represents the person. It is the heart that turns to God in repentance. It is the heart that loves God above all things, that longs for his will to be done. Our hearts were made for God, and thus, a pure heart is one that is filled with God. It is a heart that is not adulterated. It has a single purpose, one orientation, one desire. It is a heart uncluttered with anything that can lead it away from God. Jesus was saying that the person whose life is God-centered, who is looking in God's direction, will indeed see God.

Becoming God-centered depends first of all on an intimate knowledge of Jesus and his values through prayer and reflection on Jesus' life. One begins to see the contrast between the values of Jesus and the values of modern society. To be truly God-centered means living a life that is counter-cultural.

The realization that one must be counter-cultural can be a frightening thought. It is not comforting to decide deliberately to be out of step with one's own culture. The process of becoming counter-cultural is an ongoing process, accomplished in small steps as one is led by the Spirit. For example, one might realize that Jesus led a simple life with emphasis on people not things. In light of this realization, the hunger for more and more, so much a part of our U.S. consumerism, is a contrary value. Making the decision to live more simply, to conserve our dwindling resources leads gradually to a counter-cultural life style. One's mind and heart become freer and more able to center on God.

The pure of heart pray to know God's will that they may faithfully follow it, that they may remain God-centered. There are many interpretations of the phrase "God's will." Some people still think of it as a blueprint God has worked out for an individual's life from birth to death. In this context, knowing God's will simply means discovering what the blueprint looks like and trying to follow it.

Another way of looking at God's will is that our Creator is making the blueprint day by day *with us*. God's initiative urges us forward one small step at a time. Each time we respond, God is ready with another initiative. God is always very gentle with us, never using force to push us in a certain direction.

Because God's initiatives are so quiet, a

mere whisper, we need to be in tune with what God is doing in our lives. To hear the tiny whisper in which God reveals his will to us takes prayerful listening. If the whole time of prayer is spent chattering to God, God does not have a chance to reveal himself to us. A listening heart and the willingness to wait for God's time are necessary to living this Beatitude.

If we listen and wait we will recognize God in the desires he places in our hearts, in the circumstances we find in our lives, in the voices of other people, in the urgings to help another, and in the movement toward greater truth, love and reconciliation. Each choice then becomes the backdrop for God's next call. Each choice is one small step toward God. The individual focused on God is ready to hear and reply. This process of carefully listening for God we call discernment. Discerning God's will is a daily obligation, so we need to ask God for the daily bread that gives us spiritual energy.

As we are being led step by step we do not see the whole journey. At times we may feel confused and wonder if we are really becoming a God-centered person. If we continue to respond with trust in God's wisdom and goodness, the time will come when we can look back and see the road we traveled. We can then see where we have been and how God has led us to this present moment.

In the long discourse of Jesus with the Samaritan woman, he uses the symbol of a "spring of water welling up to eternal life" (Jn 4:14). Here, as elsewhere, water symbolizes the Spirit. When the Spirit fills the heart a singleness of purpose bubbles up in actions directed to God.

When the heart is pure one sees the effect of the Spirit's influence, especially in spontaneous actions. If a person has time to think about a response, his or her actions may be contaminated with manipulation, hypocrisy or cunning. When a response is spontaneous and God-centered, we know it comes from a pure heart. As Jesus told the Samaritan woman, it leaps up to provide eternal life.

Jesus promised that those who are pure of heart will see God. We do not need to wait until heaven to see God. At the Last Supper Jesus told his disciples he must soon leave them. In his distress at this announcement, Philip said, "Master, show us the Father, and that will be enough for us." Jesus assured Philip, "Whoever has seen me has seen the Father" (Jn 14:8-9). As we read and pray the Scriptures to become better acquainted with Jesus, we are sharpening our vision of the Father.

Then, Jesus promised to send the Spirit to remain with them: "I will ask the Father, and he will give you another Advocate to be with you always, the Spirit of truth, which the world cannot accept, because it neither sees nor knows it" (Jn 14:16-17).

Because of the Spirit within us, we can also see God and his activity in the people around us. Some people look at their neighbor and see faults, defects and evil. The pure of heart see the goodness of God reflected in those around them. As one lives out this Beatitude, God becomes visible in all his creation. A person begins to regain the innocence of childhood that wonders at sunsets, flowers, birds and all God's creatures.

Even in ugly things, God can be visible because he is also present there. The pure of heart look at a broken body hanging on a cross and see divinity.

"Blessed are the peacemakers,
for they will be called children of God."
(Mt 5:9)

THE PEACEMAKERS

Some of the Beatitudes seem to highlight the inner attitudes of the disciple; some stress the way a Christian should relate to others. This Beatitude definitely belongs to the second group.

Peace is almost impossible to define. It is first an inner attitude of soul, a solid centering in God that remains unshaken in the midst of turmoil. This was the message of Jesus the night before he died. After giving himself to the apostles in the Eucharist, Jesus began his last discourse with the words, "Do not let your hearts be troubled" (Jn 14:1). Knowing that the coming days would be full of distress, fear and turmoil for the apostles, Jesus urged them to have faith in God and in him. A steadfast faith is the foundation of inner peace.

Later in the same discourse, Jesus said: "Peace I leave with you; my peace I give to you. Not as the world gives do I give it to you." Then Jesus repeated, "Do not let your hearts be troubled or afraid." Having a strong faith, a person is able to receive the gift of peace that Jesus is so ready to give.

Jesus warned his disciples about mistaking the world's peace for his peace. He told them his peace is different from the peace the world gives. The peace of the world is experienced on a personal level as the nice cozy feeling we have when everything is going well for us. A truer name for this feeling is a sense of complacency, very different from the peace of Christ. The test for Christ's peace comes when things are not going well, for the peace Jesus gives does not depend on exterior circumstances.

Individual peace is important for without it there can never be peace in families, in communities or in the world. But Jesus demands more of his followers. He does not say, "Blessed are the peaceful," but "Blessed are the peace*makers*." It is one thing to possess inner peace and to rejoice in that possession. It is a much greater challenge to strive to make peace possible for others.

Peacemaking must begin in one's own

heart. Even though we know that peace is a gift of God we must also strive for peace. Our efforts involve doing everything we can do to prepare our hearts to receive God's gift.

The first step toward being a peacemaker is to be at peace with God. In writing to the Colossians, Paul quoted a hymn of the early church about Christ. The hymn ends with the lines:

> For in him all the fullness was pleased to dwell,
> and through him to reconcile all things for him,
> making peace by the blood of his cross,
> whether those on earth or those in heaven.
> (Col 1:19-20)

It is through Christ that we can become reconciled to God and able to receive the gift of peace. Christ freely gives peace "provided that you persevere in the faith, firmly grounded, stable, and not shifting from the hope of the gospel that you have heard" (Col 1:23). Uniting our efforts to God's activity, we believe that God wants us to experience the peace he offers us. Being at peace with God we are then ready to begin living this Beatitude, to become peacemakers.

Peace is much more than the absence of open conflict. Still, we must say that solving conflictual situations is often the preliminary step to real peace. Estrangement between family members, alienation of people in the same parish community, and hostility among co-workers all provide challenging situations for the peacemaker.

To be a peacemaker is to run the risk of being rejected. It takes courage and humility to bring about a reconciliation with someone who has harmed you. It takes even greater fortitude to try to make peace in the lives of people who are hostile to their family or neighbors. It is so easy to look the other way and not get involved.

Being a peacemaker involves tact and sincerity. No attempt at coercion or manipulation serves the interests of true peace. True peace comes about only by an inner change in attitude, a conversion. It means breaking down alienation and creating new ways for people to think about each other and to relate to one another.

In symbolic language Isaiah presents a delightful image of peace:

Then the wolf shall be a guest of the lamb,
and the leopard shall lie down with the kid;
The calf and the young lion shall browse together,
with a little child to guide them.

The cow and the bear shall be neighbors,
together their young shall rest;
the lion shall eat hay like the ox.
The baby shall play by the cobra's den,
and the child lay his hand on the adder's lair.
There shall be no harm or ruin on my holy mountain.
(Is 11:6-9)

As we read the prophet's description and imagine all of creation living in such harmony, we cannot help but desire peace.

But this harmony is not the result of wishful dreams or pious prayers, or even fasting. Speaking through Isaiah, God said to the Israelites:

Do you call this a fast,
a day acceptable to the Lord?
This, rather, is the fasting that I wish;
releasing those bound unjustly,
untying the thongs of the yoke;
Setting free the oppressed,
breaking every yoke;
Sharing your bread with the hungry,
sheltering the oppressed and the homeless;
Clothing the naked when you see them,
and not turning your back on your own.
Then you shall call, and the Lord will answer;
you shall cry for help, and he will say: Here I am!
(Is 58:5-7, 9)

To be a peacemaker, it is not enough to cry out to God for peace. We must unite works of justice to our earnest prayer, all the while acknowledging that peace is not the result of our work but God's gift. By our struggles for justice we prepare ourselves and others for the reception of God's generous gift.

If we want to be peacemakers we must be willing to work for justice. We must be willing to recognize unjust structures and search for nonviolent ways of changing those structures. In other words, in order to live this Beatitude we must be incorporating into our lives the challenge of the fourth Beatitude: "Blessed are those who hunger and thirst for righteousness, for they will be satisfied."

While on their missionary journey, Paul and Timothy arrived in Greece and started making converts in Philippi and Thessalonica. As a result of harassment and persecution, Paul had to leave the area. Later when Timothy reported the conditions in Thessalonica, Paul wrote to the people giving them some practical instructions for making and keeping peace among themselves. Paul asked them "to respect those who are laboring among you and . . . to show esteem for them with special love on account of their work. Be at peace among yourselves. We urge you, brothers, admonish the idle, cheer the fainthearted, support the weak, be patient with all. See that no one returns evil for evil; rather, always seek what is good both for each other and for all" (1 Th 5:12-15).

The advice of Paul is still valid today. With more respect and esteem in families, in the workplace, and more care for one another, peace would have a better chance of flourishing. It is usually the petty, irritating behavior among those who must live or work closely together that results in hostility and the loss of peace.

The peacemaker needs more than good intentions in order to establish peace in some conflict situations. Training is available in the skills needed to defuse anger, to negotiate differences, to surface unconscious fears and resentments so that the conflict is resolved without winners and losers.

On a more sophisticated level, these are some of the same skills that are needed to establish peace between nations. We can't all negotiate at an international level, but we ignore our personal responsibility for world peace at the risk of world destruction. In today's world when war can readily become the annihilation of humanity, it is crucial that we all contribute in whatever way we can to world peace. We can pray for those who make decisions about our lives and we can pressure our representatives in Congress to take action for peace.

The very presence of huge stockpiles of nuclear arms places the whole world in jeopardy. There have been numerous accidents involving nuclear warheads. Information about most of these incidents never reaches the public. Dr. Helen Caldicott in her book, *Missile Envy*, writes:

> The last declassified accident occurred in September 1980 at Damascus, Arkansas when an Air Force repairman dropped a heavy wrench socket, which rolled off the work platform and fell toward the bottom of a silo. The silo contained a Titan II missile with a nine-megaton warhead (1 megaton = 1 million tons of TNT). The socket bounced and struck the missile, causing a leak from the pressurized fuel tank. About eight and a half hours after the initial puncture, fuel vapors within the silo ignited and exploded the liquid fuel. One man was killed; twenty more

people were injured. The nine-mega-
ton hydrogen bomb was catapulted
hundreds of yards away and was found
in a field next to a grazing cow. Had the
weapon exploded, its effect would have
been approximately 720 times greater
than that of the Hiroshima bomb. (p.
292)

Relating such an incident is not meant to
be a scare tactic but it is certainly a sobering
thought that can motivate us to pray for peace
and become a peacemaker in some way. The
stakes are so high that living this Beatitude is
not an option. The survival of the world and
civilization depends on all of us creating the
conditions for God to gift us with world peace.

*"Blessed are they who are persecuted
for the sake of righteousness,
for theirs is the kingdom of heaven."*
(Mt 5:10)

THE PERSECUTED

*I*f one really takes seriously what Jesus said in
the first seven Beatitudes, the eighth Beatitude
comes as no surprise. One has only to look at
what happened to Jesus to know the results of
living his message.

As in the first Beatitude, Jesus told his
disciples that the effect of living this Beatitude
is an experience of the kingdom *now*. What
does it mean to experience the Kingdom as
present in one's life? By thinking of the Kingdom as God's presence and activity in the
world, it seems that the Beatitude person has
an experiential awareness of God. Beyond intellectual knowing, beyond the conviction of
faith, one is certain that God is a personal God
with whom one has an intimate relationship.
This relationship is dynamic, moving the

person gently to a fuller participation in the life of Christ.

Because the Jews were looking for an earthly Kingdom in opposition to the Roman rule, Jesus expanded this Beatitude so there would be no misunderstanding. Since his Kingdom would be very different from their expectations, Jesus spelled out in some detail what he meant by persecution. He said: "Blessed are you when they insult you and persecute you and utter every kind of evil against you falsely because of me. Rejoice and be glad, for your reward will be great in heaven" (Mt 5:11). He would suffer persecution and those who followed him closely must expect the same treatment.

The disciples had only to recall their own tradition to know what to expect, for all the prophets had been rejected, forced to flee for their lives and often killed for speaking a message of repentance. They were to learn that Jesus too would be rejected by the scribes and Pharisees, scorned by his own people, betrayed by one of the Twelve, denied, spit upon, flogged, condemned by the High Priest and crucified by the Romans — all because he preached the Kingdom. They would be convinced that there is no way to live and preach the message of Jesus and at the same time avoid persecution.

In his last talk with his disciples on the night before he died, Jesus tried to prepare them for the days ahead. He told them that the more they resembled him the more they would be treated just as he was treated. He said:

> If the world hates you, realize that it hated me first. If you belonged to the world, the world would love its own; but because you do not belong to the world, and I have chosen you out of the world, the world hates you. (Jn 15:18-19)

John uses the word "world" to signify the evil in the world, all that is in opposition to the message of Jesus. Jesus warned his disciples that they will experience the opposition of evil because they are alien to it. If they belonged to the world they would be accepted and praised. But since they belonged to Jesus they would receive the same treatment he received.

Here Jesus gave us the answer to the often repeated question, "Why do bad things happen to people who try so hard to follow Jesus?" Somehow we find it very difficult to accept Jesus' answer. We keep looking for the rewards of goodness in this life, forgetting what happened to Jesus and so many of his true followers down through the centuries.

Today, the disciple of Jesus must accept the fact that there is still a tie between living and preaching the Good News and suffering persecution. We would like to think that there is some other way. There was no other way for Jesus; and the true follower of Jesus is still challenged to rejoice in the opportunity to be more like him. Jesus knew how difficult it would be for us to realize the blessedness of being persecuted. He showed how his disciples must live differently than those who have no faith.

There are such a variety of responses to being insulted, rejected and persecuted. Many people spontaneously react with vengeance. They are not satisfied until they can get even with someone who has hurt them. Then there is the person who sincerely tries to live this Beatitude. This person sees persecution as an opportunity to be like Jesus and be more deeply inserted into the Kingdom.

Jesus told us we must resemble him at an even deeper level by praying for those who persecute us. He set an example for us by praying to the Father as he hung on the cross, "Father, forgive them, they do not know what they are doing" (Lk 23:24).

There is a real link between this last Beatitude and the message, "Blessed are the peacemakers." To be a peacemaker implies taking action for the Kingdom, proclaiming the message of Jesus. Anyone who has tried to be true to this call of Jesus knows that it leads to persecution.

One has only to look at Central America today to see the results of preaching the message of Jesus. As the poor peasants hear of God's love for them and reflect on the Gospel in their own lives, they begin to realize their own dignity. They are no longer willing to live in virtual slavery to the large landowners. They want to be free and they demand their human rights. When this happens the Church is accused of being subversive. Priests, sisters and lay leaders of Christian communities are arrested and tortured. They disappear and are killed all because they proclaim the Good News of God's love.

There is one caution that needs to be observed in reflecting on persecution. The persecution that Jesus was talking about is the result of living fully the message of Jesus. But people are also persecuted for many other reasons. Some are objects of hostility and ill-treatment because of their own irritating behavior. This is *not* the persecution that Jesus was talking about.

As Paul told us, being persecuted for Jesus draws a person to greater love of God. It creates a bond that is strong because it comes from Jesus. To avoid becoming self-righteous or complacent in persecution, one needs a discerning heart. One needs to ask, in the light of the Spirit, "Where is this persecution coming from? Why am I being persecuted? Because of Jesus or my own unchristian behavior?"

How surprised Paul must have been to hear those words, "I am Jesus, whom you are persecuting" (Ac 9:5). Those words changed Paul from being a persecutor to joining the persecuted. In his later letters he rejoices that he has been able to suffer for and with Christ.

At the Last Supper Jesus makes it so clear that he lives in his disciples. He prays to the Father for his disciples, "That they may be one, as we are one; I in them and you in me" (Jn 17:21). The presence of Jesus in a person who is persecuted brings inner peace. One who is suffering for the Kingdom is given an inner strength to endure. There is joy — not because one is suffering, but because one is closely united to Jesus. Then one can truly say the Kingdom is *now* just as Jesus promised.

APPENDIX A

*C*omparing several translations of a Scriptural text can often provide new insights into the meaning of the text. For your convenience, three translations of the Beatitudes are included here.

A - The Jerusalem Bible - 1966
B - Revised New Testament of New American Bible - 1986
C - New English Bible - 1972

I

A) How happy are the poor in spirit;
   theirs is the kingdom of heaven.
B) Blessed are the poor in spirit,
   for theirs is the kingdom of heaven.
C) How blest are those who know their need of God;
   the kingdom of heaven is theirs.

81

II

A) Happy are those who mourn;
   they shall be comforted.
B) Blessed are they who mourn,
   for they shall be comforted.
C) How blest are the sorrowful;
   they shall find consolation.

III

A) Happy the gentle:
   they shall have the earth for their
   heritage.
B) Blessed are the meek,
   for they will inherit the land.
C) How blest are those of gentle spirit;
   they shall have the earth for their
   possession.

IV

A) Happy are those who hunger and thirst for
   what is right:
   they shall be satisfied.
B) Blessed are they who hunger and thirst for
   righteousness,
   for they will be satisfied.

C) How blest are those who hunger and thirst
   to see right prevail;
      they shall be satisfied.

V

A) Happy the merciful:
      they shall have mercy shown them.
B) Blessed are the merciful,
      for they will be shown mercy.
C) How blest are those who show mercy;
      mercy shall be shown to them.

VI

A) Happy the pure of heart:
      they shall see God.
B) Blessed are the clean of heart,
      for they will see God.
C) How blest are those whose hearts are pure;
      they shall see God.

VII

A) Happy the peacemakers:
      they shall be called sons of God.
B) Blessed are the peacemakers,
      for they will be called children of God.
C) How blest are the peacemakers;
      God shall call them his sons.

VIII

A) Happy are those who are persecuted in the
   name of right:
   > theirs is the kingdom of heaven.
B) Blessed are they who are persecuted
   for the sake of righteousness,
   > for theirs is the kingdom of heaven.
C) How blest are those who have suffered
   persecution for the cause of right;
   > the kingdom of heaven is theirs.

APPENDIX B

I — THE POOR IN SPIRIT

Prayer Starters:

Lk 12:16-20	Ask for the grace of a deep awareness of your need of God.
1 Cor 2:6-7, 11-12	Ask the Spirit to guide you in living the values of Jesus.
Ps 4:7-9	Implore God for a joyful confidence in him.
Mt 6:26-34	Ask Jesus for an appreciation of the value of a human person.
Mt 7:7-11	Ask for the grace of greater trust in God's unconditional love for you.

Questions for Discussion:

1) Do you believe that it is good to be poor? Why or why not?
2) Besides material poverty, what other kinds of poverty have you seen?
3) Do you believe that the richest people are the happiest? Give reasons for your answer.
4) When do you feel most secure?
5) What evidence do you see that the reign of God is NOW — that God is active in creation? in your life? in history?

II — THE SORROWFUL

Prayer Starters:

Jn 2:13-17	Ask Jesus for the grace to accept your own feelings.
Jn 11:28-36	Ask Jesus to teach you how to be with another in sorrow.
Is 61:1-3	Ask for the grace to recognize and respond to grief in its many forms.
Mt 9:35-38	Entreat Jesus to give you his compassion for the poor.
Mt 26:26-46	Ask for the grace to console Jesus as you find him in those around you.

Questions for Discussion:

1) What does it mean to you to accept your own feelings?
2) Can you share an example when it was difficult for you to accept your feelings?
3) Do you believe people should be allowed to grieve or should you try to cheer them up? Give reasons for your answer.
4) In what ways are the divorced and the poor grieving? How can you show your compassion for such people?
5) What experiences have you had of being with people in other types of suffering? How did they find the consolation of this Beatitude?

III — THE GENTLE

Prayer Starters:

Jn 18:19-24	Beg God for the inner strength that comes from meekness.
Lk 22:24-27	Ask for the grace to understand success as Jesus does.
Mk 10:13-16	Beg Jesus for a deeper appreciation of children.

Ps 37:3-11   Beg for the grace to reverence
              the earth.
Dt 8:7-14   Ask Jesus to increase your faith
              in his promises.

Questions for Discussion:

1) What connection do you see between
   gentleness and trust in God?
2) Do you feel that being gentle, especially for
   a man, is a sign of weakness? Why or why
   not?
3) What is the difference between apathy and
   gentleness?
4) If children today are taught to be
   cooperative with one another, will they be
   able to survive in a competitive world?
5) What suggestions would you give a young
   family to help them deal with the tensions
   and frustrations of daily life?
6) How are those who are concerned about
   ecology and the environment really living in
   the spirit of this Beatitude?
7) Do you believe that the earth can provide
   enough food to adequately feed the world's
   population? If so, why are people starving?
8) In what ways does the United States
   resemble the Promised Land?

IV — THE JUST

Prayer Starters:

Mt 9:27-30	Beg for the grace to see your need of conversion.
Is 58:6-7	Beg for the grace to recognize oppression in the lives of others.
Is 1:15-18a	Ask God for the courage to be just.
Ep 4:1-6, 16	Beg for the Spirit to be active in your life.
Mt 13:4-9	Ask that this Beatitude may be fruitful in you.

Questions for Discussion:

1) How do you understand "conversion"? Can you give an example of a conversion experience?
2) In what ways are charity and justice alike? How do they differ? Are both necessary in our society?
3) As you think about unjust structures what examples come to your mind?
4) What unjust situations need changing in your neighborhood? in your city? in the church?

5) Do the small efforts of ordinary people make a difference in changing unjust structures? What can you do?

V — THE MERCIFUL

Prayer Starters:

Lk 18:10-14a	Plead for the grace to experience God's mercy.
Jn 20:19-21	Beg for a merciful heart like the heart of Jesus.
Jn 20:22-23	Ask to receive the Spirit more fully in your life that you may be merciful.
Lk 15:11-21	Beg for the grace to be compassionate like your Father is compassionate.
Mt 18:21-22	Beg for the grace to recognize your human limitations.

Questions for Discussion:

1) How is this Beatitude related to each of the other four?
2) Have you ever felt that being merciful was being "soft"?

3) How was Jesus' greeting of "Peace" on the evening of his Resurrection an expression of his mercy?
4) Have you ever experienced the forgiveness of another as the release of restricting bonds?
5) It has been suggested that the "Parable of the Prodigal Son" should be called the "Parable of the Merciful Father." Do you think this would be a more appropriate title for this parable? Why or why not?
6) Do you think that someone who continues to harm you should be forgiven indefinitely? If not, what is the limit of mercy?

VI — THE PURE OF HEART

Prayer Starters:

Pr 4:20-25	Beg for the grace of an uncluttered heart.
Mt 6:9-13	Entreat God for the grace to be faithful to his will.
1 K 19:11-13	Beg for a quiet, listening heart.
Jn 4:10, 13-14	Ask for the grace to know the source of your actions.
Jn 14:8-10, 15-17	Beg for the clarity of vision to see Jesus in those around you.

Questions for Discussion:

1) How do you explain the distorted ideas of the past in regard to this Beatitude?
2) What are some of the things in our modern society that tend to make hearts cluttered?
3) What are some of the practical difficulties in thinking of God's will as a blueprint? What does "God's will" mean to you?
4) "If we listen and wait we will recognize God in the desires he places in our hearts." How do you feel about this statement? Does it seem self-centered to you? Why or why not?
5) What does the symbol of water as the source of life say to you?
6) What happens to your attitudes when you try to see God in the people around you?

VII — THE PEACEMAKERS

Prayer Starters:

| Jn 14:27 | Ask for an open heart to receive the peace of Jesus. |
| Col 1:21-23 | Beg to be at peace with God. |

Is 11:4-6	Beg for the desire to be a peacemaker.
1 Th 5:12-15	Ask for the courage to take the risk of making peace.
Is 2:2-4	Beg for the grace to contribute to world peace.

Questions for Discussion:

1) How would you describe peace?
2) Can you share a time of your life when you felt really at peace? What was going on in your life at that time?
3) How do you explain the paradox that peace is a gift of God but we must work for peace?
4) Now that the U.S. is on more friendly terms with Russia, do you believe we are in any danger from nuclear weapons?
5) In what ways can you contribute to world peace? Are you convinced that these ways will make a difference? Why or why not?

VIII — THE PERSECUTED

Prayer Starters:

Jn 15:18-20	Ask Jesus for the grace to be identified with him.
Mt 5:41-46	Beg for the grace to pray for your persecutors.
Mt 5:11-12	Beg for the grace to rejoice in time of persecution.
Rm 8:35-39	Ask the Spirit for the grace of discernment.
Ac 9:1-6	Beg for a deeper awareness of the presence of Jesus.

Questions for Discussion:

1) Do you believe that a radical living of the Beatitudes will result in persecution? Explain your answer.
2) Give some examples from your own life, or a friend's, of persecution for being a Christian.
3) Why are so many priests, sisters, and lay leaders murdered in Central America? What effect do you think these deaths have on the faith of the people?

4) Reviewing all eight Beatitudes:
    a) what are some of the connecting links between the individual statements?
    b) show how an event in the life of Christ illustrates or expands a particular Beatitude.